T0395014

FUSION

Be an OSTRICH Expert

by
E. C. Andrews

BEARPORT
PUBLISHING

Minneapolis, Minnesota

Credits
All images are courtesy of Shutterstock.com, unless otherwise specified. With thanks to Getty Images, Thinkstock Photo, and iStockphoto.

Recurring – LadadikArt, Milano M, The_Pixel, yana shypova, vectorplus, NotionPic, Macrovector, In Art, Aleks Melnik, ARTvektor. Character throughout – NotionPic. Cover – Krakenimages.com, Slim Segi, In Art, Aleks Melnik, The_Pixel, Milano M, vectorplus, Macrovector. 4–5 – Susanne Russe, bruna-nature. 6–7 – Eleanor Esterhuizen, John Carnemolla. 8–9 – Ekkachai, netti, Ilya Lukichev. 10–11 – k.z, JONATHAN PLEDGER, no_limit_pictures. 12–13 – Four Oaks, Henk Bogaard. 14–15 – iModDesign, Lifes_Sunday. 16–17 – Art Konovalov, Andrea Willmore. 18–19 – Tido M, fullempty. 20–21 – Vladimir Wrangel, EcoPrint. 22–23 – Photography Phor Phun, Stacey Ann Alberts.

Bearport Publishing Company Product Development Team
Publisher: Jen Jenson; Director of Product Development: Spencer Brinker; Managing Editor: Allison Juda; Editor: Cole Nelson; Associate Editor: Naomi Reich; Associate Editor: Tiana Tran; Designer: Kim Jones; Designer: Kayla Eggert; Designer: Steve Scheluchin; Production Specialist: Owen Hamlin

Library of Congress Cataloging-in-Publication Data is available at www.loc.gov or upon request from the publisher.

ISBN: 979-8-89577-008-5 (hardcover)
ISBN: 979-8-89577-439-7 (paperback)
ISBN: 979-8-89577-125-9 (ebook)

For more information, write to Bearport Publishing, 5357 Penn Avenue South, Minneapolis, MN 55419.

CONTENTS

MEET THE BIOLOGIST

Hello! My name is Dr. Ozzy Egbert, and I am a **biologist**. I have traveled around Africa and Australia to learn all I can about ostriches. They are amazing birds!

Being an ostrich **expert** is a lot of work. I filled this notebook with everything I know about ostriches. Will you read it? Together, we can find out even more!

AN OSTRICH'S BODY

Ostriches have huge eyes on the sides of their heads. This helps them look out for **predators** without moving their heads very much! The birds also have amazing eyesight, so they can see things from very far away.

An ostrich's eye is bigger than its brain!

6

Ostriches can run faster than any other bird in the world. They can reach speeds up to 43 miles per hour (69 kph). Long and fast legs help ostriches escape from predators.

Ostriches are the only birds with two toes. However, biologists do not know why. Some think ostriches may have **evolved** this way to help them keep their balance when they run.

Ostriches have one sharp claw on each foot.

The upper body of an ostrich is covered in soft feathers. These feathers stop the birds from getting too hot or too cold. An ostrich uses the colors of its feathers as **camouflage** to hide from predators.

9

WONDERFUL WINGS

Unlike most birds, ostriches cannot fly. Their wings are not strong or big enough to lift their heavy bodies off the ground. However, ostrich wings are still very useful.

Ostriches use their wings for balance and to help them change direction when running. They also use them to protect their babies from the sun and rain.

Chicks

Baby ostriches are called chicks.

DRY HOMES

Ostriches live in Africa and Australia. They are often found in hot and dry habitats, such as deserts, open woodlands, and grasslands.

A habitat is the place where a plant or animal lives.

It can be hard for animals to find water in dry habitats. Luckily for ostriches, they have **adapted** to their challenging homes. These birds can go a long time without drinking. They get most of the water they need from their food.

Ostriches will drink from water holes when they find them.

DINNER TIME

Ostriches do not have teeth.

Ostriches are omnivores, which means they eat both plants and animals. They feed mostly on grasses, leaves, and fruits. However, the hungry birds will also eat small animals, including insects.

What else do ostriches have for dinner? Stones! Swallowing stones helps them **digest** their food by grinding it down inside their bodies. Ostriches have long intestines to make sure all their food is fully digested.

Ostriches look for stones or pebbles small enough to swallow.

15

FAMILY TIME

A group of ostriches is called a herd. Each herd has a **male** and **female** ostrich in charge. At certain times of the year, other males join the herd to have chicks with the females. But the males often leave the group later.

A male ostrich

A female ostrich

Ostriches **communicate** using different sounds. The birds might make loud hisses or squawks to warn the herd about nearby predators. But if they cannot run away fast enough, ostriches will flop to the ground and lay their heads and necks down.

Most herds have about 10 ostriches. But sometimes, they can have more than 100 birds!

ENORMOUS EGGS

Ostriches are the largest birds in the world. Because of their huge size, ostriches also lay the biggest eggs of any bird. Each female ostrich in a herd will lay its eggs in the same big, shared nest.

Ostrich eggs weigh about 3 pounds (1.4 kg). That's as heavy as a toaster!

18

Ostrich nests are shallow dips made in the dirt.

Each female ostrich can lay up to 10 eggs at a time. That means a shared nest can have as many as 50 eggs! The males and females in a herd take turns looking after the eggs.

19

LIFE CYCLE

The ostrich life cycle begins with an egg. It can take up to 46 days for babies to come out of their eggs. After a few days, the chicks leave the nest with their parents.

A life cycle includes the different stages of an animal's life.

20

Ostriches can live to up to 40 years old in the wild.

All the ostriches in a herd teach the chicks how to find food. After three to four years, the chicks grow into adults. By then, the young ostriches are ready to continue the life cycle by having chicks of their own.

ODD OSTRICHES

From swallowing stones to laying enormous eggs, ostriches are odd creatures! I hope you've enjoyed learning about these amazing birds.

You have just begun your ostrich adventure. There is so much more to learn about them. Continue to study. Soon, you'll be an expert, too!

GLOSSARY

adapted changed over time to survive in an environment

biologist a person who studies and knows a lot about living things

camouflage a covering or coloring that makes animals blend in to their surroundings

communicate to share information

digest to break down food into things that can be used by the body

evolved changed and developed over time

expert a person who knows a lot about something

female an ostrich that can lay eggs

male an ostrich that cannot lay eggs

predators animals that hunt other animals for food

INDEX